STUDIES IN ECONOMIC HISTORY

This series, specially commissioned by The Economic History Society, provides a guide to the current interpretations of the key themes of economic history, in which advances have recently been made, or in which there has been significant debate.

The series will give readers access to the best work done, help them to draw their own conclusions in some major fields and, by means of the critical bibliography in each book, guide them in the selection of further reading. The aim is to provide a springboard to further work rather than a set of pre-packaged conclusions or short cuts.

ECONOMIC HISTORY SOCIETY

The Economic History Society, which numbers over 3,000 members, publishes the *Economic History Review* four times a year (free to members) and holds an annual conference. Inquiries about membership should be addressed to the Assistant Secretary, Economic History Society, Peterhouse, Cambridge. Full-time students may join the Society at special rates.

STUDIES IN ECONOMIC HISTORY

Edited for The Economic History Society by M. W. Flinn

Enclosure and the Small Farmer in the Age of the Industrial Revolution

Prepared for
The Economic History Society by

G. E. MINGAY, B.A., PH.D.

Professor of Agrarian History
in the University of Kent at Canterbury

MACMILLAN

© The Economic History Society 1968

First edition 1968
Reprinted 1973

Published by
THE MACMILLAN PRESS LTD
London and Basingstoke
Associated companies in New York Dublin
Melbourne Johannesburg and Madras

SBN 333 03909 2

Library of Congress catalog card no. 68-27608

Printed in Great Britain by
THE ANCHOR PRESS LTD
Tiptree, Essex

Contents

Maps

Acknowledgements

I wish to acknowledge the invaluable advice of Professor H. J. Habakkuk and Dr. Joan Thirsk in formulating the views expressed in this book.

Preface

SO long as the study of economic history was confined to a small group at a few universities, its literature was not prolific and its few specialists had no great problem in keeping abreast of the work of their colleagues. Even in the 1930s there were only two journals devoted exclusively to this field. But the high quality of the work of the economic historians during the inter-war period and the post-war growth in the study of the social sciences sparked off an immense expansion in the study of economic history after the Second World War. There was a great expansion of research and many new journals were launched, some specialising in branches of the subject like transport, business or agricultural history. Most significantly, economic history began to be studied as an aspect of history in its own right in schools. As a consequence, the examining boards began to offer papers in economic history at all levels, while textbooks specifically designed for the school market began to be published.

For those engaged in research and writing this period of rapid expansion of economic history studies has been an exciting, if rather breathless one. For the larger numbers, however, labouring in the outfield of the schools and colleges of further education, the excitement of the explosion of research has been tempered by frustration caused by its vast quantity and, frequently, its controversial character. Nor, it must be admitted, has the ability or willingness of the academic economic historians to generalise and summarise marched in step with their enthusiasm for research.

The greatest problems of interpretation and generalisation have tended to gather round a handful of principal themes in economic history. It is, indeed, a tribute to the sound sense of economic historians that they have continued to dedicate their energies, however inconclusively, to the solution of these key problems. The results of this activity, however, much of it stored away in a wide range of academic journals, have tended to remain inaccessible to many of those currently interested in the subject. Recognising the need for guidance through the burgeoning and confusing literature that has grown around these basic topics, the Economic History Society decided to launch this series of small books. The books are intended to serve as guides to current interpretations in important fields of economic history in which important advances have recently been made, or in which there has recently been some significant debate. Each book aims to survey recent work, to indicate the full scope of the particular problem as it has been opened up by recent scholarship, and to draw such conclusions as seem warranted, given the present state of knowledge and understanding. The authors will often be at pains to point out where, in their view, because of a lack of information or inadequate research, they believe it is premature to attempt to draw firm conclusions. While authors will not hesitate to review recent and older work critically, the books are not intended to serve as vehicles for their own specialist views: the aim is to provide a balanced summary rather than an exposition of the author's own viewpoint. Each book will include a descriptive bibliography.

In this way the series aims to give all those interested in economic history at a serious level access to recent scholarship in some major fields. Above all, the aim is to help the reader to draw his own conclusions, and to guide him in the selection of further reading as a means to this end, rather than to present him with a set of pre-packaged conclusions.

University of Edinburgh
Spring, 1968

M. W. FLINN
Editor

The Problem

TOWARDS the end of the nineteenth century, in a period of considerable difficulties for landlords and farmers and of a steady flow of labourers from the land, there was a growing public concern with the decline of the English peasantry. The realisation grew that the English agrarian structure had become markedly different from that of the Continent, and that the peasantry proper, the small owner-occupiers, has fallen to a very low ebb. In 1887, to be precise, only about 12 per cent of the occupiers of agricultural land were the owners of it (although if the occupiers who owned a part of their land were included the figure would rise to 16 per cent). Many of these surviving owner-occupiers were in fact substantial commercial farmers, or were small owners who had their main occupation outside agriculture, and so the English peasantry seemed to have been absorbed among the 900,000 agricultural labourers, numbers of whom were abandoning the soil in which they had no rights or interest and from which they obtained but a meagre living.

It was these circumstances, and the growth of the radical land reform movement of the later nineteenth century, that stimulated historians' interest in discovering just when and why the English agrarian structure assumed its modern form, and the period was one rich in scholarly investigation and discussion.[1] From the pioneering days of Thorold Rogers a hundred years ago, the lost peasantry of England became a main theme of agrarian history, and a list of those scholars who have engaged in the discussion would be very long and would include some of the greatest names in our historiography – Tawney, Gay, Gray, the Hammonds and Ernle, to mention but a few.

The learned debate has continued to the present and has attracted major contributions from modern scholars such as Habakkuk, Hoskins, Chambers, and Joan Thirsk, among many

[1] For a discussion of some of the relevant literature see G. E. Mingay, Introduction to E. C. K. Gonner, *Common Land and Inclosure* (2nd edn., 1966).

others.[1] This continued interest in so old a subject springs not merely from the fascination exercised by a controversial and still unsolved problem, but because the decline of the peasantry is central to the study of agrarian change and, it has been argued, to that of industrial change also. However, before we enter into the complexities of the subject it will be necessary to define more precisely just what it is we are discussing, and what questions we are attempting to answer.

We may begin by suggesting that the term 'peasantry' is best abandoned at the outset: it is too imprecise and too charged with romantic and sentimental overtones. The same objections may be lodged against the word 'yeoman'. While historians have usually been careful to limit the meaning of yeoman to owner-occupiers, writers of the seventeenth, eighteenth and nineteenth centuries observed no such rule but applied it as a broad indication of status, including within its usage not only owner-occupiers large and small (from 'yeomanly Gentry' to the 'statesmen' or small-holders of the north), but tenant-farmers, leaseholders, and copyholders as well; moreover, by the eighteenth century the term had spread into commerce and industry (we hear of yeoman brewers, bakers, carpenters and bricklayers, coal-merchants and coal-masters), and also into the armed forces. In this pamphlet we are concerned with the decline of the *small farmer*, a category which includes both owner-occupiers and tenant-farmers, and since some of the changes we shall discuss affected owners and tenants in different ways we shall try to avoid confusion by eschewing 'peasant' and 'yeoman', and refer rather to owner-occupiers and tenant-farmers – recognising the complication that some farmers were in fact both, owning a part of their land and renting the remainder.

Although great scholars such as Tawney and Gay concerned themselves with earlier developments, the major centre of interest in the controversy over small farmers tended to focus on the era of parliamentary enclosure between about 1760 and 1830. More than anything, perhaps, this was due to the influence of Marx and his indication of the key significance of enclosure in his account of 'the genesis of the capitalist farmer'; but it arose also from the supposed close relationship between parliamentary enclosure, contemporary changes in farming methods, and the

[1] For details see the Bibliography.

development of industry in the later eighteenth century, a relationship discussed by Marx, Toynbee, Mantoux, and more recently Maurice Dobb. Marx indicted enclosure as the instrument by which the landlords, following up their earlier 'thefts of State lands' carried out a 'systematic robbery of the communal lands' of the people with the object of creating large capitalist farms and setting free 'the agricultural population as proletarians for manufacturing industry'.[1] Subsequent writers followed Marx's lead and studied in detail the Enclosure Acts and Awards and the extensive eighteenth-century literature on the subject. In the years before 1914 a half-dozen major studies by Slater, Levy, Hasbach, Gonner, Ernle, and the Hammonds, treated this period in detail, and while diverging in approach, seemed to confirm that the vital connexion between the agrarian changes and the decline of the small farmer was to be found in the era of parliamentary enclosure. However, not all scholars agreed with this conclusion, even at this time, and as we shall see, modern opinion tends to side with them.

The question of when the small farmer declined most rapidly is, of course, central to this discussion. But to that we must add two other essential questions, and the problem may be set out as follows:

(1) *To what extent* did the small farmer decline? What indications are there of the actual fall in numbers and acreage occupied?
(2) *When* did the small farmer decline? Was the crucial period that of the parliamentary enclosures and post-Napoleonic Wars depression, or was it earlier?
(3) *Why* did he decline? In what ways was the small farmer adversely affected by enclosure and changes in farming methods, and was he also affected by other and possibly more important factors?

None of these questions is easy to answer, and to a large extent the answers we can give must be regarded as provisional, or at least expressible only in guarded terms. But the major conclusion that will emerge is that the evidence provided by modern authorities does not, on balance, support the views that were generally accepted and taught by the former generation of agrarian historians.

[1] K. Marx, *Capital* (English edn., 1886), pp. 461–3.

11

The Extent of the Decline

NO exact or even very approximate answer to the first of our questions can be given because the essential information required for such an answer does not exist. We are driven back to more or less impressionistic guesses derived from the estimates of Gregory King and the imperfect government statistics of the nineteenth century. We may be fairly sure, however, that the extent of the decline in the 150 years before 1900 was much less than was believed by the earlier historians, who were misled by the supposed severe effects of the enclosure movement and technical developments in farming, and by the polemics of eighteenth-century pamphleteers. They may have been misled also, as Clapham suggested, by some narrowing in the early nineteenth-century use of the term 'yeoman': this was then coming more nearly to coincide with the historians' limited sense of 'owner-occupier', and this was occurring at a time when the holders of such obsolete tenures as leases for lives and copyholds of inheritance (formerly included among the yeomen) had recently been, or were still being, bought out by their landlords and their tenancies exchanged for annual agreements or leases for terms of years.[1] The supposed 'disappearance of the yeomen' may thus have arisen in part from confusion over the meaning of the term and a certain decline among the categories of land-holders who once came within its meaning.

That there was any disastrous decline of small farmers after the early eighteenth century is in fact improbable. The belief that a very great decline occurred in the later eighteenth century rests on an exaggerated view of the effects of enclosure and the technical advantages of large units; this was encouraged by contemporary writers, but is contradicted by the evidence now available. While it is still generally accepted that technical changes in farming (including the labour-intensive new rotations, the laying down of arable to leys or temporary grass, introduction

[1] J. H. Clapham, *Economic History of Modern Britain*, i (1926), pp. 99–100.

of better and more extensive breeds of livestock, and the gradual adoption of machinery) were more readily adopted by farmers of capital than by small men, it is doubtful how far the economies of scale in agriculture were important before the middle nineteenth century. Further, the changes in the markets for agricultural produce do not point uniformly in the same direction. The growing importance of livestock and livestock products, both in the markets and in the management of the soil, favoured the large graziers and mixed farmers; but a great deal of rearing was done by small men in upland areas, and dairying was essentially the business of the family farmer. Moreover, with the growth of industrial towns in the eighteenth and nineteenth centuries the markets for specialities suited to a small acreage tended to grow: vegetables, fruit, poultry, eggs, milk, hops and hay all offered opportunities to the small man with a good location and a suitable soil. On the other hand, the great increase in the area of waste lands brought into cultivation during the period – the chalk downs and limestone wolds, the marshes, heaths and large areas of rough grazing, tended to shift the balance of farm sizes because such land required time and capital to bring it into production and was usually, therefore, farmed in large units. Again, it was a general matter of good estate policy for landlords and their agents to create larger farm units – which were more easily administered, conveniently-worked, and more profitable – by amalgamating small holdings when the opportunity occurred; and the era of enclosure of course offered numerous opportunities for just this, although practical considerations necessarily limited the extent of the possible changes.

In general, the balance of forces was working in favour of larger farm units, although in any particular area the influence of local markets, soils, climate and relief might encourage a trend in the contrary direction. In any event, the growth of larger farms was not fatal to small farmers, as the nineteenth-century statistics confirm, and it is wrong to suppose that any sweeping or sudden change in farm sizes occurred, or was even possible in the conditions of the period.

When we turn to the statistical evidence we are prevented by its scarcity and incomparability from drawing any precise conclusions, but on the whole it does seem to bear out the view just expressed. Gregory King, the famous statistician of the late seventeenth century, estimated in 1688 that there were 40,000

15

freeholders of 'the better sort', and 140,000 freeholders of 'the lesser sort' (his 'freeholders' presumably including the lessees for lives and the copyholders), and 150,000 farmers, i.e. 330,000 in all, with the freeholders, it will be noted, exceeding in number the tenant-farmers. How many of the total were not small farmers at all it is impossible to say. Certainly some large-scale producers would be included, and possibly also small producers of less than twenty acres and some small absentee owners. If we guess that as high a proportion as two-thirds of the total were really small farmers of between about 20 and 100 acres then there would have been some 220,000 of them.

No exact comparison of King's figures with the nineteenth-century ones is possible, but at the census of 1891 nearly 224,000 people in England and Wales returned themselves as farmers and graziers, a figure which shows a reduction of a third on King's total of 330,000. How many of the farmers and graziers of 1891 could be classed as small farmers? In 1895 statistics of holdings showed that over 83,000 holdings exceeded 100 acres and could be regarded as medium-sized and large farms; on the basis of the census returns, therefore, small farmers probably numbered some 140,000. This figure is broadly confirmed by the 1895 statistics which showed there to be 129,000 holdings of between 20 and 100 acres. A fall from a conjectural 220,000 small farmers in 1688 to some 130–140,000 in the 1890s (representing a decline of rather less than 40 per cent) is of course considerable, but may overstate the case. At all events it is clear that even if the small farmers had declined considerably they were still numerous at the end of the nineteenth century, and the total of small farmers of between 20 and 100 acres still much outnumbered the farmers of more than 100 acres.

The decline of the small farmers since King's day, it seems evident, was a fairly limited one; the decline of the *owner-occupiers*, on the other hand, appears to have been more dramatic. A recent study by Dr. Thompson suggests that a revision of King's figures would give the owner-occupiers about a third of the income from land at the end of the seventeenth century. Clapham estimated that in 1887 only about 12 per cent of the cultivated land of England and Wales was in the hands of working owner-occupiers, while Thompson's estimate for the 1870s is only about 10 per cent.[1] Recent estimates of the proportion of the cultivated

[1] F. M. L. Thompson, 'The Social Distribution of Landed Property

acreage in the hands of owner-occupiers at the end of the eighteenth century agree fairly closely in giving them then only between 10 and 20 per cent of the total.[1] Clapham's estimate above was 12 per cent of a larger cultivated area, so that it appears that no considerable change could have occurred in the nineteenth century, and we are left with the conclusion that the major fall in the area occupied by small owners must have occurred before the later eighteenth century.

As we shall see, modern evidence on enclosure and other agrarian changes indicates that the decline of both owner-occupiers and of small farmers in general was probably not very great in the interval between the later eighteenth and the middle nineteenth centuries (contrary to what some of the early writers, such as Levy and the Hammonds, supposed). So it seems likely that there was some considerable decline between the later seventeenth century and the late eighteenth century, a decline which after a respite for small owners between the 1780s and about 1815 continued slowly in the nineteenth century. But it is to this question of the period of decline that we must turn next.

At this point, however, we may sum up the evidence so far:

(1) The small farmers (defined as having between 20 and 100 acres) were still numerous in the late nineteenth century, having well over a half of all the holdings of over 20 acres. In 1895 there were 129,000 holdings of between 20 and 100 acres; Gregory King's total of 330,000 freeholders and farmers in 1688 no doubt included a substantial number of large holdings, and probably numerous holdings of less

---

in England since the Sixteenth Century', *Econ. Hist. Rev.*, 2nd series, XIX (1966), pp. 513–14. See also Addenda, p. 42.
[1] G. E. Mingay, *English Landed Society in the Eighteenth Century* (1963), pp. 23–6; H. J. Habakkuk, 'La Disparition du Paysan Anglais', *Annales*, XX, 4 (1965), p. 655. My figure of 15–20 per cent was arrived at by deducting the estimated shares in the total acreage of the other classes of landowner. The land tax returns for some of the midland counties indicate that 11–14 per cent of the land was owner-occupied in 1802–4; the Property Tax figures, however, show that in 1808 about 18 per cent of the annual value of land was that of small owners. (It may be that the figure of 18 per cent is in excess of the actual proportion of acreage owned, since the property of small owners was likely to have a high proportion of buildings to acreage and was probably of more than average annual value per acre.)

than 20 acres. There was a general trend during the two centuries in favour of larger farm units, but there is no evidence that the decline of small farms was very rapid or sweeping, or applied to all areas.

(2) The small owner-occupiers had only 10–12 per cent of the cultivated acreage in the later nineteenth century and a not very much larger percentage in the late eighteenth century. Gregory King thought there were 180,000 free-holders (including leases for lives and copyholders) at the end of the seventeenth century – more than the number of farmers. Most of the freeholders were of 'the lesser sort', but it seems clear that King believed they had considerably more than 12 per cent of the total acreage in 1688. Thompson's estimate gives the owner-occupier a third of the income from land in King's day; a major decline must have occurred, therefore, in the hundred years from 1688.

(3) The general conclusion to be drawn is that small farmers in general declined, but certainly did not disappear; those small farmers who owned their land did decline drastically, apparently between the later seventeenth and the later eighteenth centuries.

The Period of Decline

MOST of the earlier historians of agrarian change believed that the decline of small farms was most severe and rapid in the era of parliamentary enclosure between about 1760 and 1815. For example:

> when in the second half of the century the rapid consolidation of small holdings into large farms began, the indignation which broke out and the importance ascribed to the movement point to the conclusion that till that time no tendency to increase the size of farms had been noticeable.[1]

The combination in the later eighteenth century of a supposed 'agricultural revolution' which, it was believed, profoundly affected farming methods, and enclosure, which rapidly replaced

[1] H. Levy, *Large and Small Holdings* (Cambridge, 1911), p. 3.

surviving common fields by enclosed farms more suited to the new farming, seemed to provide, in the sweeping and dramatic nature of the changes involved, many grounds for thinking that there necessarily followed a corresponding revolution in farm sizes and farm occupiers. However, much of the modern research on the period has tended to emphasise, on the contrary, how limited was the character of the changes that occurred, and it is now accepted that most of these changes had a long history of gradual development going back long before 1760 and continuing long after the end of the French wars. In other words, the modern view that the decline of the small farmers was in general a slow and protracted affair is reinforced by an appreciation that the 'agricultural revolution' itself was really a long-drawn-out process of change, and that in general the effects of the parliamentary enclosures were by no means so sweeping as was once supposed.

The 'agricultural revolution' was not simply the rural counterpart of the transition to industrialism, the agrarian side of the medal of the 'industrial revolution': it was rather a long-term process of reorganisation and change in land-use, accompanied by expansion of the cultivated area, that made possible a greater output without making a correspondingly larger demand on the labour supply. Seen in this light, the 'agricultural revolution' stretched over a number of centuries rather than decades; and indeed went back as far as the development of systems of convertible husbandry and strengthening of animal husbandry, with consequent effects on the supply of manure and improved fertility of arable soils, in the late middle ages.[1] Convertible husbandry broke down the old rigid separation of arable and grass in the midlands of the sixteenth century, even among the strips of common-field farmers; and in the seventeenth century the practice of laying down arable to temporary grass, and the introduction of nutritious legumes such as clover and sainfoin, as well as turnips, laid the foundation for a new form of land-use – one especially adapted to light soils, some of which had never even seen the plough.[2]

[1] For a more detailed discussion see J. D. Chambers and G. E. Mingay, *The Agricultural Revolution 1750–1880*, ch. 1.
[2] W. G. Hoskins, 'The Leicestershire Farmer in the Sixteenth Century', *Studies in Leicestershire Agrarian History* (Trans. Leics. Arch. Soc., 1948), and 'The Leicestershire Farmer in the Seventeenth Century', *Agricultural History*, XXV (1951); E. L. Jones, 'Agriculture

The advances in ley-farming and the adoption of rotations which included legumes and roots thus long predates the eighteenth century: the 'Norfolk system' was indeed well entrenched in that county long before the days of the celebrated 'Turnip' Townshend and Coke of Holkham. The improvement of breeds of cattle and sheep also has a long history, and the pioneer breeders of the eighteenth century (of whom Bakewell was only the most famous) achieved their somewhat limited successes with animals that had already been subject to experiment and improvement. The advantages of enclosed and compact farms, under one man's sole control, over the dispersed and fragmented holdings in common fields were widely appreciated. The common fields, of course, were subject to rights of common grazing, a restricted rotation, and the danger of disease among beasts grazed in common; nevertheless, there is plenty of evidence that the open-field farmers were not impervious to the influence of improvement. The ancient system often showed a remarkable degree of vitality, the owners and farmers co-operating in increasing the number of fields in order to permit the introduction of roots and grasses into the rotation, enclosing pieces of common-field and waste for additional pasture, and exchanging lands in order to obtain more compact and easily-worked holdings. The area left in bare fallow was reduced, and leys, i.e. land put down to grass or legumes for a period of years and then ploughed up for a succession of corn crops, were found in both open fields and closes serving the dual purpose of increasing pasturage and restoring fertility.[1]

It is clear that the 'new' farming methods so often associated with the period of parliamentary enclosure were well established in many areas, even in common-field villages, long before 1760. Full-scale enclosure, when it came, often represented the final rather than the first stage in the process of reorganisation, and its effects on farming methods and on the village community were not always very great. Frequently, parliamentary enclosure was the logical conclusion of the piecemeal creation of separate closes from the waste and the gradual modification of the common

---

and Economic Growth in England 1660–1750: Agricultural Change', *Jour. Econ. Hist.*, XXV (1965).

[1] For a survey of these developments see Chambers and Mingay, *op. cit.*, pp. 48–52.

fields that had been going on for a century or more. The object of the enclosure Act was sometimes merely to get rid of the last rump of the open fields and commons, or to confirm an enclosure carried out previously by agreement among the owners, or to complete the exploitation of the waste and tidy up an inconvenient and confused accumulation of small closes. The farming itself was not always much affected: the general effect was to extend or intensify the local specialisation that was determined by natural factors; many farmers had already a large proportion of enclosed land and had already adopted leys, legumes and roots, and in arable areas the nature of the soil did not always allow the farmers to depart from the ancient two crops and a fallow. Until the era of cheap under-drainage and the introduction of roots suited to heavy soils (such as the mangold) in the middle nineteenth century, the cold wet clay lands could not be adapted to the new husbandry, and on these soils the ancient rotations long survived enclosure.

It should not be assumed, however, that historians have been entirely mistaken in attaching so much importance to parliamentary enclosure. It meant a rapid accession to the cultivated area of large tracts of commons and waste, and for the common fields a rapid conversion to the conditions necessary for more efficient farming. Not all villages had made much progress in adjusting their common-field farming to take advantage of the new possibilities of greater fertility and greater output: Young's strictures on the 'goths and vandals' of the common fields and his view, expressed as late as 1809, that 'the old open-field school must die off before new ideas can become generally rooted'; must have had some considerable justification in the conservatism of small farmers.[1] The common-field system was wasteful, expensive, and difficult to work so long as dispersed holdings, common grazing rights, and sharing of the commons remained its basis. Enclosure offered a means of rapid transformation to lower costs per acre, higher yields, and greater profits on a larger cultivated area. It was profitable to landlords, whose increase in rents usually represented a return of 15–20 per cent or more on the outlay, and it must have been correspondingly profitable to the farmers whose greater productivity allowed them to pay much increased rents. The concentration of enclosure in periods

[1] A. Young, *General View of Oxfordshire* (1809), pp. 35–6.

of rising prices show that it was considerably influenced by the desire of landowners and farmers to take advantage of the market more readily and more completely than could be done under the limitations of the common fields, and the number of enclosure Acts— some 3,000 in the two periods of heavy activity in the 1760s–70s and 1793–1815 – gives some indication of the scale of the change.

Parliamentary enclosure thus gave a sharp fillip to improved methods of farming where conditions allowed them to be adopted. There seems little doubt, too, that generally the improved farming was more suited to farms of at least a moderate size (say above about 100 acres) and to farmers commanding capital. The question therefore arises of how far the more rapid changes in farming techniques associated with the concentrated enclosure activity of the period 1760–1815 led to widespread changes in farm sizes. (See Maps on pages 44 and 45.)

This is not an easy question to answer in simple terms because so much depended on the local conditions of soil, relief, and climate, and on the objects for which a particular enclosure was undertaken. It is important to remember first that the area affected by enclosure was largely limited to the midlands and northern counties, and that by no means the whole of this area was affected; so often the supposed effects of enclosure are discussed as if they were national rather than regional or local phenomena. Second, the areas least affected were likely to be the northern upland and midland forest areas where enclosure was very largely of waste. Here the population was small, waste land was plentiful, and the general nature of the farming – rearing and small-scale dairying – was unlikely to be much changed by enclosure. Many of the farmers in these areas were small freeholders, and they could often draw on an industrial by-employment to supplement their holdings. In the lowland areas, however, where common fields were still the basis of much of the farming, enclosure was a more serious problem: waste land was often scarce, the population was relatively large, and small freeholders held only a small proportion of the land. Farming was a full-time business, and the small freeholders and cottagers depended for employment on the larger tenant-farmers. In these conditions enclosure might well prove unfavourable to small farmers, and especially so where there was a drastic change in land-use. Thus, enclosure which resulted in conversion of common-field arable to permanent pasture for fattening probably meant a decline of small farms because fat-stock production required a heavy investment in beasts and a slower turnover of capital than with arable.

Even within the lowland area there were large areas of waste to be enclosed in the eighteenth century, mainly rough hill grazing land on the Yorkshire and Lincolnshire wolds, the Chilterns, and the Downs, land which could be ploughed up for corn. The new farms so created required farmers of capital because the breaking-up and cultivation of such land involved much labour and the full returns of the investment took time to appear. Especially during the French wars, a great deal of the enclosure activity was concerned with the bringing into production of marginal lands; and between 1793 and 1815 a million acres of waste and commons were enclosed by Acts, in addition to that enclosed by agreement. The landlords who initiated this expansion of cultivation set out to attract farmers of capital by offering a large acreage at a low rent on a long lease. Sometimes, as a result of the enclosure of waste, a number of small farmers were forced out or suffered severely from the loss of free sheep pastures. But, in general, the effects of this kind of enclosure were limited because the local population was small; the balance of farms was disturbed, not so much because small farms disappeared, but because large farms were created where none existed previously.

The main impact of enclosure, therefore, was likely to be felt in the lowland area of common fields and mixed farming. But even here the effects were often of a limited kind. Although in some areas there was conversion of arable to permanent pasture, in general the cultivation was improved rather than trans-formed; and an existing farm structure was less easily modified than was a sparsely settled area where farms were few or non-existent. It is important to understand that inequalities in land-ownership and in the size of farms had already appeared within the common-field village; indeed, it is probable that in many cases enclosure merely reinforced, rather than initiated, an old tendency towards larger farm units and sharper social divisions. On the other hand, it is obvious that a large-scale enclosure would give landlords a good opportunity for carrying out a radical change in farm sizes at the same time as land holdings were reallocated and made more compact. This engrossing was facilitated by the powers provided in enclosure Acts for the termination of leases, and it is possible that the compensation paid to leaseholders on the cancellation of their leases was used by them to stock larger farms. Landlords tended to favour large tenants because estate management was simplified and the outlay on buildings reduced. Small owner-occupiers, it has often been argued, were seriously affected by the high costs of the enclosure itself, while the compensation of the tithe-holder (often a large lay landlord) and the substitution of small pieces of land for the former common rights left the small owner with an acreage too small to be worked without access to a common, and perhaps even too small to be worth the heavy expense of fencing.

These old assertions about the results of enclosure have been subject to some re-examination in recent years. We need to be clear right at the start, however, about an important distinction. The tendency of landlords to favour larger farm units affected small *tenants*, not owner-occupiers (unless, of course, owner-occupiers rented some land – as a number did – which was amalgamated by landlords into large farms); on the other hand, the cost of enclosure, and the reduction in size and usefulness of holdings, affected the small *owner-occupiers* (and also the small absentee owners) – tenants bore no share in the costs of enclosure.

Those who have studied contemporary estate records have found that enclosure was not always such a valuable opportunity for the amalgamation of small tenancies as has often been supposed. It had long been the policy of landlords to engross small or inconvenient holdings when possible, but this process was essentially a long-term one since landlords did not generally wish to incur the odium of making changes harmful to small farmers; rather, they sought to preserve their reputation as good landlords – a point that had obvious political advantages – by not disturbing satisfactory tenants until the head of the family died or the farmers themselves agreed on a reorganisation. Moreover, the availability of farmers with capital, capable of taking on a large farm, necessarily limited the landlords' ability to create larger units. Landlords expected farmers to provide their own working capital, and the amount involved was not inconsiderable: £2 per acre was regarded as a minimum figure, or four times the annual rent. This meant that medium-sized and large farms required tenants boasting a capital in livestock, implements, and cash of some £300 upwards, and there is plenty of evidence that the scarcity of such men made landlords anxious not to risk

22

losing the occupiers of their existing large farms.[1] It follows that with a combination of landlords' reluctance to disturb small tenants unnecessarily, and the shortage of farmers with sufficient capital to stock large farms, progress towards larger farm units was a work of patience and time, and the adjustments possible at an enclosure might in practice be quite limited.

Modern opinion does not support the view of the Hammonds that the process by which an Act of Enclosure was obtained and executed was deliberately rigged against the small owner. On the contrary, careful investigators such as Gonner, and more recently Tate, have been impressed by the care taken to do justice to all who could prove rights of ownership. Indeed, it has been remarked that 'parliamentary enclosure represented a major advance in the recognition of the rights of the small man'.[2] However, the expenses of an enclosure may have often been a serious matter for the small owners. The level of costs varied considerably from place to place according to the extent and complexity of the changes involved. While in many cases the costs might only amount to a few shillings per acre, there was a tendency, however, for the average costs to rise considerably during the later eighteenth century. The costs reached a peak during the French wars, as parliamentary and commissioners' fees were increased and the length of time required to complete the work grew when more difficult parishes with large numbers of small proprietors were tackled. Supplementary expenses in connexion with new farmhouses, roads, internal fences, and drainage might outweigh the direct costs of the enclosure itself, and in some cases proprietors avoided these charges by deferring the improvements indefinitely, although this meant that some of the advantage of enclosing was lost.

A recent study shows that in Warwickshire the costs (omitting those for fencing) rose from an average of 11s. per acre before 1760 to 34s. in the 1790s, and to nearly 62s. after 1801. The average total costs for the small proprietors amounted to about £3

[1] See G. E. Mingay, 'The Size of Farms in the Eighteenth Century', *Econ. Hist. Rev.*, 2nd ser., XIV (1961–2), pp. 473–9.

[2] E. C. K. Gonner, *Common Land and Inclosure* (2nd edn., 1966), pp. 72, 73, 82, 94–5; W. E. Tate, 'Opposition to Parliamentary Enclosure in Eighteenth-Century England', *Agricultural History*, XIX (1948), pp. 137, 141–2. For a discussion see Chambers and Mingay, *op. cit.*, pp. 85–8.

per acre.[1] Costs on this scale might be a heavy burden, but were not insuperable. It was open to the small owner to raise the sum required by mortgaging his land or by selling off a few acres, and the considerable increase in the capital value of land after enclosure would make this an attractive course. A more serious problem for the very small owner in the midlands was the loss of acreage suffered in many enclosures. A serious loss of land often arose through the compensation of the tithe-holder, although as a result, of course, the small owner's remaining land was free of tithes. The inclusion of former waste and commons in the holdings might offset this, but with the disappearance of the commons went the pasturage which was frequently essential for the working of the small post-enclosure holdings. Enclosure in the densely populated midlands, where wastes and commons were limited in extent, must often have resulted in smaller rather than larger post-enclosure holdings, and in the creation of small holdings which were difficult or impossible to work.[2] Further, the expenses of fencing very small acreages could be disproportionate to the value of the land. For these reasons small owners might well decide to sell out, but there are grounds for thinking that many of those who sold out were in fact absentee owners; the owner-occupiers were generally increasing in number, and in some areas they were buying more land.

The conclusion that, on the whole, small owner-occupiers were not very severely affected by enclosure is borne out by studies of the land tax assessments. Davies showed that in the heavily-enclosed counties of Leicestershire, Warwickshire, Nottinghamshire, Derbyshire, and Lindsey, the owner-occupiers increased both in number and in acreage owned over the period 1780–1832 (although a slight downward trend was evident after 1802), and subsequent writers have confirmed and amplified his findings.[3] The land-tax evidence, although difficult to interpret

[1] J. M. Martin, 'The Cost of Parliamentary Enclosure in Warwickshire', *Univ. Birmingham Hist. Jour.*, IX (1964), pp. 146–50, 155–6.

[2] W. G. Hoskins, *The Midland Peasant* (1957), pp. 164, 249–51.

[3] E. Davies, 'The Small Landowner, 1780–1832, in the Light of the Land Tax Assessments', *Econ. Hist. Rev.*, I (1927); see also the bibliography. A recent study of enclosure in Warwickshire shows that in the early years of parliamentary enclosure the parishes affected were mainly those where small owners were strong, and indeed the small owners frequently initiated the enclosure. In these parishes

24

in detail, leaves no doubt that on balance small owners could not have been severely affected by parliamentary enclosure or by the post-1813 fall in prices; and past enclosure costs were only one factor in the burden of mortgage debt which forced some small owners to sell out in the difficult period after the French wars. The period of parliamentary enclosure was one of rising and general (but not ininterrupted) prosperity for farmers, and while some occupying owners sold out, others bought land and engaged in improvements, encouraged by the high farming profits that could be realised and by the steep increase in the value of land.

The land tax evidence also shows, however, that already in 1780 small owner-occupiers had fallen to very small numbers in large areas of the counties examined. In Oxfordshire Gray found that the occupying owners who paid from 6s. to £20 a year in tax occupied only 9 per cent of the county, while Davies found that in the 1,395 parishes he examined some 90 per cent of the land was in the hands of tenant-farmers.[1] Because of the technical difficulties of interpreting the figures these calculations should not be taken too literally, but there can be no doubt that in many areas small owner-occupiers were few in number before the most intensive period of parliamentary enclosure. We must therefore go further back to see just when, and why, the small owners – and perhaps small farmers in general – declined, to an age not generally thought of by the earlier historians as one of great or sudden agrarian changes.[2]

greater differentiation between the successful freeholders and the small owner was apparent, and the latter tended to decline. From the 1780s the parishes mainly affected by enclosure were those dominated by large landowners; here there was an increase in the number of owner-occupiers, connected with the extension of commercial tenant-farming. J. M. Martin, 'The Parliamentary Enclosure Movement and Rural Society in Warwickshire', *Agric. Hist. Rev.*, XV (1967), pp. 19–39.

[1] H. L. Gray, 'Yeoman Farming in Oxfordshire from the Sixteenth Century to the Nineteenth', *Quart. Jour. Econ.*, XXIV (1909–10), p. 301; Davies, *op. cit.*, p. 110.

[2] A. H. Johnson, the first scholar to use the land tax assessments, concluded that 'by far the most serious period for the small owner was at the close of the seventeenth and during the first half of the eighteenth century . . . and the changes since the middle of the eighteenth century have not been nearly so radical as they have been generally supposed to be'. *The Disappearance of the Small Landowner*

The Seventeenth and early Eighteenth Centuries: the Causes of Decline

THE land tax investigations have emphasised three main features of the small owner-occupiers in the late eighteenth century: they occupied only a small proportion of the land (some 10 per cent in the counties examined); they were outnumbered by the small absentee owners – who indeed were twice as numerous as the small occupying owners; and last, the small owner-occupiers were usually very few in old-enclosed parishes, i.e. parishes enclosed by agreement before the era of parliamentary enclosure.

There are several explanations of the last feature, the near-disappearance of small owners in old-enclosed parishes. It has been pointed out that landowners would naturally tend to enclose first those parishes with fewest small owners, because such parishes offered less difficulty and the best prospect of reaching an agreement among a small number of owners; further, it was an object of landowners to buy up small properties as they came on to the market in order to increase their local influence, to make existing farms more compact and efficient, and to prepare the way for an enclosure. The small proprietors might therefore be considerably reduced in number *before* the enclosure was undertaken. On the other hand, there is evidence that the relationship between early enclosure and few small owners did not always hold good, and further, that when landowners were building up their estates they bought more frequently from absentee owners rather than owner-occupiers, since the former were usually more ready to sell. It is believed that much of the land that was enclosed by agreement in the hundred years before 1760 was best suited to grass, and there was some conversion from arable to grass, a change usually thought to be adverse to the survival of small farms; yet here again instances can be found

(1909), p. 147. However, Johnson's evidence, and that of Gray and Davies, has made little impression on the general view of the problem until quite recent years.

of the survival of numerous small owners in some early-enclosed parishes under grass in the later eighteenth century.

However, there seems enough clear evidence to establish a general connection between early enclosure, the location of the parish and the nature of the soil, conversion to pasture, and a paucity of small owners. This suggests that the greater returns available from pasture farming on land not naturally well-suited to arable encouraged owners to concentrate on the enclosure of such parishes before the rise in grain prices in the later eighteenth century, and that in this process small owners were bought out either as a preliminary or as the result of the process. No doubt the technical factors of soil and land-use played a large part, but in recent years the importance of other long-term factors has been suggested. Inheritance customs, it has been argued, may have had an important influence. Small owners, in contrast to large ones, were often in the habit of dividing their property among heirs – a practice that would tend, of course, to the multiplication of small holdings. The practice of gavelkind survived in Kent, as is well known. (To some extent, however, the tendency towards a parcelling-up of small properties was offset by arrangements commonly made among the heirs to consolidate the land again in one person's hands, so that the overall trend might be quite limited.) More evidence is required to establish how widely the division of land among heirs was customary elsewhere in the eighteenth century. It seems probable that partible inheritance remained strong in forest and pasture areas, where additional land in the form of waste was still available, and where the produce of a small holding could be supplemented by earnings from mining, quarrying, and handicraft work.

The division of small properties among heirs may help to explain the existence of large numbers of small absentee owners in the later eighteenth century, since land would come into the hands of daughters and younger sons who moved away from the family home to marry or take up some trade or profession. But another and probably more important factor was the general expansion in this period of trade, industry and the professions. Younger sons of small landowners increasingly turned to these expanding fields of employment and profit for a living, and some owner-occupiers sold land in order to participate in trade or industry. When land was inherited by a younger son, or perhaps more especially by a daughter, there was a tendency to sell because it was inconvenient to manage land at a distance, and the capital could be more profitably used in the business of the son or husband. A market for small properties existed since landlords, as we have noted, were willing to buy in order to build up a compact estate or improve their farms, perhaps with an eventual enclosure in view.

Between 1660 and 1740 numbers of newly-rich families – merchants, war financiers and contractors, professional men – were trying to establish themselves among the gentry and were ready purchasers of land that would help to build up an estate. The larger established owners were on balance much more purchasers than sellers, because the growth of strict family settlements and the ease of borrowing on mortgage meant that only rarely were large owners obliged to put land up for sale.[1] In the same period, the smaller gentry and freeholders were under pressure: there were large increases in the burden of taxation, mainly connected with the wars of the period, while farming profits fell as agricultural production tended to outstrip the growth of markets. The long-term fall in agricultural prices began in the 1650s, although there were wild upward swings in years of dearth. As landlords decided that to lease out their land to large tenant-farmers was more profitable than leasing it to small copyholders or than farming the land themselves, the copyholders for lives or terms of years were forced out in favour of capitalist farmers who could farm for the market more productively. After 1660, however, even those with secure titles to land were affected. With a generally low and uncertain price level, falling farm profits, and a heavy burden of taxation, many small gentry, freeholders and copyholders of inheritance were forced to sell; while others decided that this was a good time to abandon farming for something more profitable.[2]

The gentry, however, felt less pressure to sell land in the middle eighteenth century as the burden of taxation declined and prices improved. In this period, newcomers seeking land were sometimes obliged to acquire it in piecemeal fashion, beginning

[1] See H. J. Habakkuk, 'English Landownership 1680–1740', *Econ. Hist. Rev.*, X (1940); G. E. Mingay, *English Landed Society in the Eighteenth Century* (1963), ch. II.

[2] H. J. Habakkuk, 'La Disparition du Paysan Anglais', *Annales*, XX, 4 (1965), pp. 650–4, 658–9, 662.

perhaps with a suitable farmhouse for a residence and gradually extending the estate by buying out the neighbouring freeholders. In the middle and later eighteenth century, too, the area affected by estate-building activities widened. Earlier it had affected mainly the home counties because of the need for easy access to London where the newcomers' wealth was principally generated. As new industrial areas and centres of trade developed rapidly, so the demand for gentry estates and small properties became more widely dispersed, while the high cost and scarcity of land in the home counties encouraged would-be purchasers to look further afield.

Low and fluctuating agricultural prices for more than a hundred years before 1750, combined with heavy taxation, especially between 1688 and 1715, appear therefore as crucial factors in the decline of copyholders and freeholders.[1] The decline occurred in a period when landownership trends were unfavourable to small proprietors, when opportunities in commerce, industry and the professions were expanding, when newcomers from these fields were seeking to build up estates, and when the larger owners were amassing more land in their hands and only rarely had to put land on the market themselves. But to what extent was this an unfavourable period, not merely for small owners, but for small farmers in general? Low prices and heavy taxation would affect, of course, all farmers to some degree (except that tenant-farmers were not usually required to meet the burden of the land tax); but for tenant-farmers the difficult conditions were considerably alleviated by the fall in rents after about 1670, and by the other forms of assistance frequently given by land-lords to enable their tenants to keep their farms.

However, in areas of mixed farming where production was mainly for the market small farmers were less likely to survive a difficult period than were large ones. This was partly because they lacked the financial resources of the large farmer, but also because they were more easily replaced and landlords were less likely to grant them large rent reductions or other assistance. More important, probably, was the fact that in most forms of arable and mixed farming the small farmers were less efficient, having higher costs of cultivation in relation to their acreage and output. This was the general view of contemporary agricultural

[1] *Ibid.*, p. 663.

writers, and indeed it was pointed out that a process of consolidation of small farms had been going on for a long time. 'It does not follow that if no enclosures were made, no consolidation of farms would take place', wrote Thomas Davis in his *General View of Wiltshire*.[1] 'The contrary is the fact; small estates, whether held by lives, or at rack rent, are every day consolidating in the parishes where open fields remain.' Thomas Stone, too, said in 1787: 'In almost every common-field parish the number of farms has been considerably reduced within twenty or thirty years.'[2]

These assertions are supported by a small but growing weight of documentary evidence relating to estates in Nottinghamshire, Staffordshire, Bedfordshire and Sussex, covering both common-field and enclosed farms. In the course of the eighteenth century small farms between 21 and 100 acres were halved in number, while farms of over 100 acres were correspondingly increased.[3] The present evidence suggests that the major part of this trend towards larger farms occurred in the first half of the eighteenth century, and was the result of gradual adjustments by landlords with the object of obtaining more compact and easily worked holdings, as well as larger ones. The generally low prices of the period seem to have made it difficult for many small farmers to pay their rents, and eventually they gave up or were removed by the landlord, and their holdings divided up among their more efficient neighbours.

More research is needed to ascertain how far back this process of the weeding-out of inefficient small men can be traced, and to what extent it may be related to local conditions of soils and markets and to types of farming. Present evidence suggests that on the heavy clays of the midlands the small farmers were particularly vulnerable, their costs of cultivation and of transport made high by the nature of the soil, which also had the effect of restricting the possibilities of intensifying and diversifying the output. Soil, however, was not the only and perhaps not the chief determinant; the whole spectrum of farming systems and local circumstances needs to be examined. Thus the areas of

[1] p. 49.
[2] T. Stone, *Suggestions for rendering the Inclosures . . . a source of population and Riches* (1787), p. 41.
[3] For details see G. E. Mingay, 'The Size of Farms in the Eighteenth Century', *Econ. Hist. Rev.*, 2nd ser., XIV (1961–2), pp. 480–4.

small-scale pasture farming, where the cultivators' subsistence holdings were supplemented by industrial earnings, were probably much less affected by price trends and engrossing. There is no doubt that some areas were more favourable to the survival of small farmers than others; and that where they were numerous in the eighteenth and earlier centuries they were generally still strong in the later nineteenth century. When the various areas of survival have been studied in detail it may be possible to say more positively just why the small farmers declined or survived.

Conclusion

WE may now sum up and see what answers we are able to provide for the three questions with which we began:

(1) *The extent of the decline*: the available statistics can give us no accurate idea of the extent of the decline of small farms in general, but certainly small farms were still numerous in the late nineteenth century, perhaps mainly in the areas where for natural reasons they had always been strong. They did not disappear, therefore, although for technical and commercial reasons the long-term trend was in favour of larger units. Over the country as a whole the small owner-occupiers had already declined to possession of a very low proportion of the cultivated acreage in the later eighteenth century (probably some 11–14 per cent); and they had only a slightly lower proportion in the late nineteenth century; their main decline certainly predates the later eighteenth century.

(2) *The period of decline*: modern understanding of the slow pace of the 'agricultural revolution' and of the effects of parliamentary enclosures does not, in general, support the old view that a major decline of small farmers occurred between 1760 and 1830. The land tax evidence, indeed, shows that the numbers of small owners tended to rise for much of this period. Some engrossing of farms occurred, but it was limited by the practical difficulties of displacing small farms in large numbers. The major decline of small owners and of small farmers in general must have occurred before 1760, probably between about 1660 and 1750.

31

(3) *The reasons for decline between 1660 and 1750*: the period was one of generally low prices, and taxation was heavy between 1688 and 1715. In some areas of mixed farming and production for the market small tenant-farmers failed and their holdings were amalgamated into larger units. The growth of alternative occupations in trade, industry, and the professions made small farms less attractive both as an occupation and as an investment. A good market for small properties was provided by the large landlords who were extending their estates and enclosing, and by newcomers seeking to establish themselves among the land-owning classes. Small farmers remained strong in some areas, probably because incomes from small-scale dairying and rearing could be supplemented by industrial earnings.

This study began by reminding readers that historical interest in the decline of small farmers was influenced in the later nine-teenth century by the realisation that in Europe, unlike England, a peasantry had survived (and indeed survives still, to the concern of governments troubled by low incomes and low productivity in agriculture). Wisely or not, English agrarian historians, with few exceptions, have studied the English problem in isolation from its wider European context. Long ago, A. H. Johnson made a tentative approach to a broader line of attack, but his lead has not been followed up. Perhaps, after all, we should give priority to the exploration of matters still obscure in our own agrarian history, such as the existence of regional variations in the decline of small farmers, the importance of inheritance customs, and of price movements. Much more research is needed to establish the role of these and other factors. On the other hand, it would certainly be instructive to examine the reasons why small farmers have survived in much greater numbers in continental Europe, and to consider what relevance these may have for the English experience; but this will not be a light undertaking, and is obviously beyond the scope of the brief discussion presented here.

Select Bibliography

The place of publication is London, unless otherwise stated.

I   The 'Agricultural Revolution'

J. D. Chambers and G. E. Mingay, *The Agricultural Revolution 1750–1880* (1966). The most up-to-date and comprehensive survey of the agrarian changes of the period. Chapter 4 presents the modern view of the enclosure movement.

G. E. Fussell, 'From the Restoration to Waterloo', Introduction to Lord Ernle, *English Farming Past and Present* (6th edn. 1961). Good on the innovations and technical changes, but little or nothing on landownership, enclosure, and other aspects.

G. E. Fussell, 'Low Countries' Influence on English Farming', *English Historical Review*, LXXIV (1959). The best and most detailed discussion of this subject.

E. L. Jones, 'Agriculture and Economic Growth in England 1660–1750: Agricultural Change', *Journal of Economic History*, XXV (1965). Primarily concerned with the development of convertible husbandry on the light soils in the century before 1750.

G. E. Mingay, 'The Agricultural Revolution in English History: a Reconsideration', *Agricultural History*, 37 (1963) Reprinted in Charles K. Warner, *Agrarian Conditions in Modern European History* (N.Y. 1966), and in *Essays in Agrarian History*, II (ed. W. E. Minchinton, 1968). A brief survey (with numerous references) of the idea and literature of the 'agricultural revolution', and a discussion of recent research and findings.

R. A. C. Parker, 'Coke of Norfolk and the Agricultural Revolution', *Economic History Review*, 2nd Series, VIII (1955–6). An important article which shows that the 'Norfolk system' was well established on Coke's estates long before his time, while Coke himself was important for fostering other agricultural developments.

R. Trow-Smith, *English Husbandry* (1951). A most useful

35

general survey of the changes in crop husbandry and livestock, but with relatively little on other matters.

R. Trow-Smith, *History of British Livestock Husbandry 1700–1900* (1959). The standard work on the subject, and indispensable for a full understanding of it.

II   Regional Studies

J. D. Chambers, *Nottinghamshire in the Eighteenth Century* (2nd edn. 1966). A classic regional study, with valuable discussions of the role of the squirearchy, industry, and poor law, as well as agriculture.

J. D. Chambers, *The Vale of Trent* (Supplement No. 3 to *Economic History Review*, 1957). A penetrating study of the course of industrialisation, incorporating much new research, and dealing particularly with the population changes, industry, and agriculture of an area important in the early stages of the industrial revolution.

C. Stella Davies, *The Agrarian History of Cheshire 1750–1850* (Manchester, 1960). Contains some useful material from primary sources, but weak in interpretation and on the relationship to the agrarian changes as a whole.

David Grigg, *The Agricultural Revolution in South Lincolnshire* (Cambridge, 1966). A comprehensive, up-to-date, model survey of the changes in a limited area, written with a strong geographical bias, distinguished by a wide use of sources and sound understanding of the historical aspects.

Alan Harris, *The Open Fields of East Yorkshire* (E. Yorks. Local History Society, 1959). A brief local study which brings out the variety and flexibility of open-field farming.

M. A. Havinden, 'Agricultural Progress in Open-Field Oxfordshire', *Agricultural History Review*, IX (1961). A valuable discussion of progressive open-field farming, particularly on the introduction of sainfoin and turnips for feeding larger numbers of beasts, resulting in turn in a larger supply of manure.

W. G. Hoskins, 'The Leicestershire Farmer in the Sixteenth Century', in *Studies in Leicestershire Agrarian History* (Transactions Leics. Arch. Society, 1948); 'The Leicestershire Farmer in the Seventeenth Century', *Agricultural History*, XXV (1951). These two studies by Hoskins are invaluable for understanding the true nature of open-field husbandry, and the flexibility of the system as it developed before the period of parliamentary enclosure.

W. G. Hoskins, *The Midland Peasant* (1957). A detailed study of the development of one Leicestershire village (Wigston Magna), particularly relevant here for its account of the changing social structure before and after enclosure.

E. L. Jones, 'Eighteenth-century changes in Hampshire Chalk-land Farming', *Agricultural History Review*, VIII (1960). An account of the introduction of convertible husbandry in the free-draining chalk hills of Hampshire.

R. Molland, 'Agriculture c. 1793–c. 1870', *V.C.H. Wiltshire*, IV (1959). A well-rounded account of mid-nineteenth century developments in the varied agricultural regions of Wiltshire, one of the backward, low-wage counties.

Joan Thirsk, *English Peasant Farming* (1957). A detailed account of the agricultural development of Lincolnshire, stretching from the seventeenth to the nineteenth centuries, and soundly based on the natural regions of a large and diverse county.

Joan Thirsk, *V.C.H. Leicestershire* II (1954). A thoughtful and balanced discussion of seventeenth- and eighteenth-century farming in a county famous for its livestock husbandry.

Olga Wilkinson, *The Agricultural Revolution in the East Riding of Yorkshire* (E. Yorks Local History Society, 1956). An interesting brief survey, particularly useful for its discussion of enclosure.

III Major Aspects of the Decline of Small Farmers

A. W. Ashby, *Allotments and Smallholdings in Oxfordshire: A Survey* (Oxford, 1917). Primarily concerned with the small-holdings movement of the late nineteenth and early twentieth centuries, this is useful for the light it throws on the factors influencing the success or failure of small producers.

J. D. Chambers, *Nottinghamshire in the Eighteenth Century* (2nd edn. 1966). Chapter 7 discusses the effects of enclosure on rural population and employment, and stresses that much depended on local types of soil and the husbandry carried on; it was found that many small owners had been bought out before enclosure.

J. H. Clapham, *Economic History of Modern Britain*, I (1926), ch. 4; II, ch. 7. These chapters from the standard work on the nineteenth century discuss in detail the evidence for the decline of the yeomanry, the sizes of holdings and numbers of farmers at various dates, the value of common rights, and the availability of gardens and allotments. They provide a vital statistical corrective to more impressionistic and dramatic accounts of the agrarian changes.

P. G. Craigie, 'The Size and Distribution of Agricultural Holdings in England and Abroad', *Journal of the Royal Statistical Society*, L (1887). Useful mainly for the detailed figures of distribution by counties of holdings in the nineteenth century; these show that many small holdings survived even in the heavily enclosed counties.

E. C. K. Gonner, *Common Land and Inclosure* (2nd edn. 1966, with Introduction by G. E. Mingay). A major work, dull and dreary, but indispensable for its balanced account of the procedure and effects of enclosure, and how it was affected by geographical factors. The statistical treatment is probably unreliable, and the account of the decline of small farmers does not take account of the land tax evidence. The Introduction reviews the contribution of Gonner and other writers, notably the Hammonds, Slater and Levy, and indicates where Gonner's findings have been modified by more recent research.

H. J. Habakkuk, 'English Landownership 1680–1740', *Economic History Review*, X (1940). The key article on changes in landownership before the age of parliamentary enclosure, on which much further research has been based. It argues that, in this period, large estates with their greater resources grew at the expense of the smaller gentry and freeholders.

H. J. Habakkuk, 'La Disparition du Paysan Anglais', *Annales*, XX, 4 (1965). A review (in French) which goes back to the sixteenth century, and stresses the importance of changes in economic conditions, particularly prices and taxation, the growing opportunities outside farming, and, from the middle eighteenth century, the rising demand for small estates created by newcomers to the gentry.

H. J. Habakkuk, 'The English Land Market in the Eighteenth Century', in *Britain and the Netherlands* (ed. J. S. Bromley and E. H. Kossmann, 1960). This treats a more specialised aspect of the changes in landownership and demand for estates; it considers particularly the effects of fluctuations in taxation and rates of interest, and the availability of mortgages, in determining the supply and the price of land.

A. H. Johnson, *The Disappearance of the Small Landowner* (new edn. Oxford, 1963, with Introduction by Joan Thirsk). An early work that contradicted the popular view established by the Hammonds; now largely outdated, but valuable still for its general discussion of the problem and the relevance of the land tax evidence. Joan Thirsk's Introduction suggests some new lines of enquiry that remain to be followed up.

G. E. Mingay, *English Landed Society in the Eighteenth Century* (1963). A general survey, the first of its kind, of the structure, nature and changes in landed society. Chapters 2–4 consider the factors in the growth of large estates and decline of small ones in the period, and provide the background for this subject.

G. E. Mingay, 'The Size of Farms in the Eighteenth Century', *Economic History Review*, 2nd ser., XIV (1961–2). This essay argues the case for a secular growth of larger farm units, but points out also those factors (landlords' conservatism and concern for welfare and political support, the shortage of tenants capable of stocking large farms, etc.) which limited the growth trend and made for a degree of stability in farm sizes (despite the opportunities for change provided by enclosure).

F. M. L. Thompson, *English Landed Society in the Nineteenth Century* (1963). An excellent survey of the position of the large owners and gentry and the forces influencing their social and political strength in the nineteenth century. The book forms a logical continuation of the study of the landed classes in the eighteenth century by G. E. Mingay, above.

F. M. L. Thompson, 'The Social Distribution of Landed Property in England since the Sixteenth Century', *Economic History Review*, 2nd ser., XIX (1966). The main relevance of this valuable article is the discussion of the validity of the figures provided by Gregory King and others for the distribution of land among the social classes at various dates. See reference on page 14.

IV   Enclosure

For further bibliography see W. H. Chaloner, 'Recent Work on Enclosure, the Open Fields, and related Topics', *Agricultural History Review*, II (1954).

T. S. Ashton, *An Economic History of England: the Eighteenth Century* (1955). Chapter 2 deals with agriculture in general, and is particularly important for its discussion of the influence of the rate of interest on enclosure.

J. D. Chambers, 'Enclosure and Labour Supply in the Industrial Revolution', *Economic History Review*, 2nd ser., V (1952–3). An article of the first importance, discussing the Marxist view that enclosure led to depopulation and provided the labour supply for early industrialisation. Chambers concludes that enclosure increased employment, but the effect of population growth in both open and enclosed villages was to create a surplus of rural labour that agriculture, although expanding, could not absorb; it was from this surplus that the industrial labour force grew.

J. D. Chambers, *Nottinghamshire in the Eighteenth Century* (2nd edn. 1966). Chapter 7 of this work is referred to in the preceding section. Chapter 6 discusses the influence of types of soil and tenure on enclosure, and compares the result where land was concentrated in a few hands and where it was widely distributed.

J. D. Chambers and G. E. Mingay, *The Agricultural Revolution, 1750–1880* (1966). Chapter 4 gives the most up-to-date detailed survey of the enclosure movement.

W. H. R. Curtler, *The Enclosure and Redistribution of our Land* (Oxford, 1922). Probably the most useful general survey of the subject, and one that is objective in its approach. As much more research has been done since it was published it needs to be read in conjunction with recent works, e.g. Chambers and Mingay, *The Agricultural Revolution, 1750–1880*, and R. A. C. Parker's *Enclosures in the Eighteenth Century* (see below).

E. C. K. Gonner, *Common Land and Inclosure* (2nd edn. 1966, with Introduction by G. E. Mingay). See 'The Period of Decline' p. 23 above.

David Grigg, *The Agricultural Revolution in South Lincolnshire* (Cambridge, 1966). Particularly useful for the role of enclosure in technical changes in part of Lincolnshire, with some discussion of the effect on small farmers and the reasons for their survival. See also 'The Extent of the Decline', pp. 12 ff. above.

J. L. and B. Hammond, *The Village Labourer* (1912). The best-known and most readable account of eighteenth-century enclosure and its impact on the village; now regarded as dangerously biased and largely superseded by more recent research. It still deserves to be read as a classic of historiography, but read also the critique in G. E. Mingay's Introduction to

E. C. K. Gonner, *Common Land and Inclosure*. See 'The Period of Decline', p. 23 above.

W. G. Hoskins, *The Midland Peasant* (1957). See 'The Extent of the Decline', pp. 12–16 above.

H. G. Hunt, 'The Chronology of Parliamentary Enclosure in Leicestershire', *Economic History Review*, 2nd ser., X (1957–8). Discusses the factors affecting the timing of parliamentary enclosure in Leicestershire, with particular emphasis on the distribution of landownership as a factor.

V. M. Lavrovsky, 'Parliamentary Enclosure in the County of Suffolk (1797–1814)', *Economic History Review*, VII (1937); 'Tithe Commutation as a Factor in the Gradual Decrease of Landownership by the English Peasantry', *Economic History Review*, IV (1933). A technical discussion, based on a small sample of enclosures, of the effects of tithe commutation and consolidation of rented land into large farms on the survival of small freeholders who, before enclosure, farmed rented land in addition to their own.

Hermann Levy, *Large and Small Holdings*, translated by R. Kenyon (2nd edn. 1965). A very old work, only partly concerned with eighteenth-century enclosure, and now completely outdated. Its argument that, owing to high prices for corn, large farms grew to the extinction of old ones, is highly exaggerated and misleading. See the critique in G. E. Mingay's Introduction to E. C. K. Gonner, *Common Land and Inclosure*, and 'The Period of Decline', p. 23 above.

J. M. Martin, 'The Cost of Parliamentary Enclosure in Warwickshire', *University of Birmingham Historical Journal*, IX (1964). An important new addition to the literature, which shows that enclosure costs rose considerably in the course of the later eighteenth century; and so in the later enclosures the expenses may have had serious effects on the small proprietors. (See p. 23.)

J. M. Martin, 'The Parliamentary Enclosure Movement and Rural Society in Warwickshire', *Agricultural History Review*, XV, 1 (1967). A recent and detailed discussion, mainly important for the stress placed upon the different effects of enclosure in upland areas of small population, plentiful waste land, and dairy farming, as compared with those in lowland areas of denser population, limited waste, and a husbandry primarily based on open fields. (See p. 24.)

R. A. C. Parker, *Enclosures in the Eighteenth Century* (Historical

Association Aids for Teachers No. 7, 1960). An excellent discussion of the problem in a small compass. For a fuller discussion of many of the points raised here see Chambers and Mingay, *The Agricultural Revolution, 1750–1880*, ch. 4.

G. Slater, *The English Peasantry and the Enclosure of Common Fields* (1907). An early work of limited usefulness and now almost entirely superseded. See the critique in G. E. Mingay's Introduction to E. C. K. Gonner, *Common Land and Inclosure*, and p. 23 above.

W. E. Tate, 'Opposition to Parliamentary Enclosure in Eighteenth-Century England', *Agricultural History*, XIX (1948); 'Parliamentary Counter Petitions during Enclosure of the Eighteenth and Nineteenth Centuries', *English Historical Review*, LIX (1944). Two important articles which provide a useful corrective to the account of parliamentary procedure on enclosure Bills in the Hammonds' *Village Labourer*. Tate considers that the legal claims of small owners were justly treated, and that the opposition to enclosure was relatively small.

W. E. Tate, 'The Cost of Parliamentary Enclosure in England (with special reference to the County of Oxford)', *Economic History Review*, 2nd ser., V (1952–3). Tate found the average cost of 38 enclosures in Oxfordshire to be only 27s. 6d. per acre; his findings should be compared with those of Martin for Warwickshire (see above), where the costs rose considerably in the later eighteenth century.

W. E. Tate, *The English Village Community and the Enclosure Movement* (1967). A recent book which revises the figures for numbers of enclosure Acts and acreages enclosed, but adds little else to present knowledge. It is useful as an introduction to the subject, especially for the amateur local historian, but the interpretation of the effects of enclosure is partial and unbalanced.

Joan Thirsk, *English Peasant Farming* (1957). Deals with the varying chronology and effects of enclosure in the diverse natural regions of Lincolnshire, and relates enclosure to soil, population and landownership factors.

V The Land Tax

J. D. Chambers, 'Enclosure and the Small Landowner', *Economic History Review*, X (1940). A brief statistical study of the land tax evidence for the effects of enclosure in the east midlands.

E. Davies, 'The Small Landowner 1780–1832, in the Light of the

Land Tax Assessments', *Economic History Review*, I (1927). The first detailed statistical investigation of the land tax assessments carried out on a large scale, with a discussion of its value as a source, this article has inspired and influenced a number of subsequent investigators. Davies's finding that small owners occupied only a small proportion of the land in 1780, but increased in number and acreage between 1780 and 1802, has very important implications for the enclosure controversy. Some recent writers (see below) believe that he under-estimated the difficulties of using the assessments and that his detailed findings, as distinct from his broad conclusions, may be invalid.

H. L. Gray, 'Yeoman Farming in Oxfordshire from the Sixteenth Century to the Nineteenth', *Quarterly Journal of Economics*, XXIV (1909–10). An early investigation of the assessments, which are used to quantify the changes in owner-occupied land in Oxfordshire. The results here should be compared with those of Davies for other counties.

D. B. Grigg, 'The Land Tax Returns', *Agricultural History Review*, XI, 2 (1963). A new study of the assessments for south Lincolnshire which shows a relationship between natural farming regions and the survival of owner-occupiers. This might be compared with Chambers' discussion of the same relationship in Nottinghamshire. (See *Nottinghamshire in the Eighteenth Century*, ch. 6). Grigg also points out some of the weaknesses of the land tax as a source, and considers that Davies's method of calculating an acreage-equivalent of the tax for a whole county is invalid.

H. G. Hunt, 'Landownership and Enclosure 1750–1830', *Economic History Review*, 2nd ser., XI (1958–9). Uses the land assessments to study the influence of concentration of landownership on enclosure, and how far enclosure, in turn, affected landownership. There was a general trend for land to be transferred from small to large owners, although in the war period the decline in small owners occurred among absentees, not owner-occupiers. There is a brief discussion of the difficulties of using the assessments.

G. E. Mingay, 'The Land Tax Assessments and the Small Landowner', *Economic History Review*, 2nd ser., XVII (1964–5). This is a critique of Davies's use of the land tax as a source, emphasising (1) the lack of a constant relationship between the assessment and the acreage, and (2) the fact that many small owners rented additional land, so that the total size of their farms did not correspond to the acreage deduced from the tax assessments.

J. M. Martin, 'Landownership and the Land Tax Returns', *Agricultural History Review*, XIV (1966). This is in the nature of a rejoinder to the criticisms outlined above, Martin considering that in strictly rural areas the assessments provide an accurate guide to acreage, although he does not discuss the error arising from the renting of additional land by owner-occupiers.

Joan Thirsk, *V.C.H. Leicestershire*, II (1954). Uses the assessments to outline changes in landownership in Leicestershire. The results here should be compared with those of Hunt above.

W. R. Ward, *The English Land Tax in the Eighteenth Century* (Oxford, 1953). A general study of the administration and political implications of the tax, this is not concerned with the use of the assessments for examining changes in landownership.

Addenda

Since the above Bibliography was completed several valuable books and articles on agrarian history have appeared:

E. L. Jones (ed.), *Agriculture and Economic Growth in England 1650–1815* (1967), is concerned with a more limited subject and period, and contains in addition to the editor's introduction seven valuable papers, including four of those listed above.

Sheila Lambert, *Bills and Acts: Legislative Procedure in Eighteenth-Century England* (1971). This work contains a valuable discussion of Enclosure Bills, and shows that Parliament was concerned that these and other private Bills were given proper scrutiny and publicity: an important corrective to the Hammond version of Parliament's attitude to enclosure.

Donald N. McCloskey, 'The Enclosure of Open Fields: Preface to a Study of its Impact on the Efficiency of English Agriculture in the Eighteenth Century', *Journal of Economic History*, XXXII, 1 (March 1972). This is an attempt to measure the improvement in agricultural efficiency brought about by the enclosure of open fields, using the methods of the 'new economic history'. However valid the conclusion, the discussion is of considerable interest.

W. E. Minchinton (ed.), *Essays in Agrarian History* (2 vols., Newton Abbot, 1968), contains 24 important essays from a variety of journals (including a number of the articles listed above), covering the whole era from the appearance of the manor to the present century.

Michael E. Turner, 'The Cost of Parliamentary Enclosure in Buckinghamshire', *Agricultural History Review*, XXI, 1 (1973), makes the important point that since substantial enclosure costs were often incurred after the commissioners' completion of the award, previous estimates of the average costs have been too low.

J. G. Brewer, *Enclosures and the Open Fields: A Bibliography* (British Agricultural History Society, 1972). This publication, obtainable from the British Agricultural History Society, Museum of English Rural Life, The University, Reading, Berkshire, contains the most up-to-date bibliography on the subject.

A recent discussion by J. P. Cooper considers further King's figures, and reinforces the view that the freeholders were thought of as having a very substantial proportion (at least 25 per cent) of the land in the later seventeenth century: 'The Social Distribution of Land and Men in England, 1436–1700', *Econ. Hist. Rev.*, 2nd series, XX (1967), pp. 431–40.

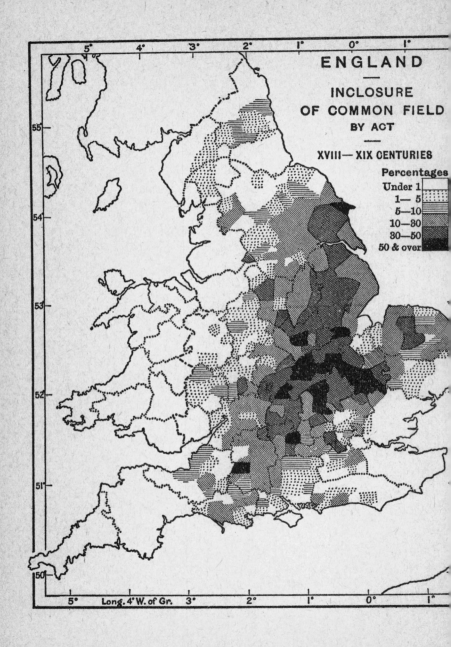

ENGLAND

—

INCLOSURE
OF COMMON FIELD
BY ACT

—

XVIII— XIX CENTURIES

Percentages
Under 1
1— 5
5—10
10—80
30—50
50 & over

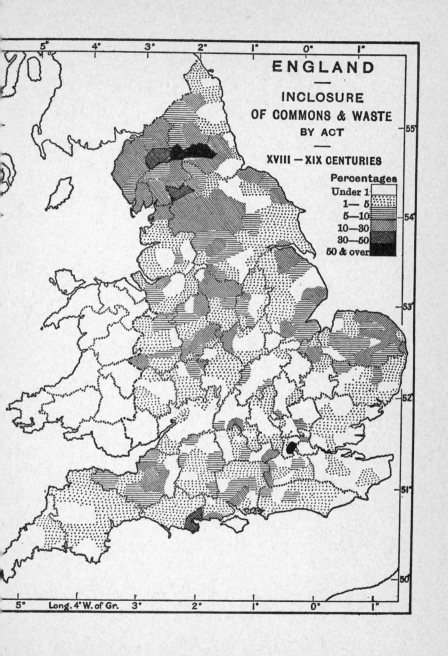

ENGLAND
—
INCLOSURE
OF COMMONS & WASTE
BY ACT
—
XVIII — XIX CENTURIES

Percentages
Under 1
1— 5
5—10
10—30
30—50
50 & over

Long. 4° W. of Gr.

Index

Absentee owners, 14, 22, 24, 26, 27
Agricultural revolution, 16–18, 31

Bakewell, Robert, 18

Chambers, J. D., 9, 17 n., 18 n., 23 n.
Clapham, J. H., 12, 14–15
Coke of Holkham, 18
Common fields, 18–19, 20–1, 30
Convertible husbandry, 17–18
Cooper, J. P., 15 n.
Copyholders, 10, 28–9

Davies, E., 24–5
Davis, Thomas, 30

Enclosure, 10, 11, 16, 18–25, 32; and engrossing, 20–1; and improved farming, 19–20; and owner-occupiers, 23–5, 26–7; costs of, 22–3, 25
Engrossing of farms, 13, 20–3, 24, 26, 30; and enclosure, 20–1
Ernle, Lord, 11
Estates, development of, 21, 22, 26, 28–9, 30, 32

Farmers' capital, 22–3
Farms, size of, 13, 20–3
Freeholders, 14, 16, 20, 28–9. *See also* Owner-occupiers

Gentry, 28–9
Gonner, E. C. K., 9 n., 11, 23
Gray, H. L., 9, 25

Habakkuk, H. J., 9, 15 n., 28 n.
Hammond, J. L. and B., 9, 11, 15
Hasbach, W., 11
Hoskins, W. G., 9, 17 n., 24 n.

Inheritance customs, 27–8

Johnson, A. H., 25 n., 32
Jones, E. L., 17 n.

King, Gregory, 12, 13, 14, 15–16

Land tax, 24–5, 26, 31
Leaseholders, 10, 14, 22
Levy, H., 11, 15, 16

Martin, J. M., 24 n., 25 n.
Marx, Karl, 10–11
Mingay, G. E., 15 n., 17 n., 18 n., 23 n., 28 n., 30 n.

Norfolk system, 18

Owner-occupiers, 9, 14–16, 22–3, 25, 26–7, 30. *See also* Freeholders

Slater, G., 11
Stone, Thomas, 30

Tate, W. E., 23
Tenant-farmers, 10, 20, 22–3, 32
Thirsk, Joan, 9
Thompson, F. M. L., 14, 16
Tithes, 22, 23
Townshend, 'Turnip', 18

Yeoman, 10, 12
Young, Arthur, 19